THE QUOTABLE
WINSTON CHURCHILL

A COLLECTION OF WIT AND WISDOM

Running Press
PHILADELPHIA • LONDON

A Running Press® Miniature Edition™

© 2013 by Running Press

All rights reserved under the Pan-American and International Copyright Conventions

Printed in China

9   8   7

Digit on the right indicates the number of this printing

Library of Congress Control Number: 2012954809

ISBN 978-0-7624-4983-5

Running Press Book Publishers
A Member of the Perseus Books Group
2300 Chestnut Street
Philadelphia, PA 19103-4371

Visit us on the web!
www.runningpress.com

the earth to join in the fight for freedom. After the conflict's end, he was the first to fully comprehend the new dynamics of the Cold War world—he coined the term "Iron Curtain," dedicated himself to trans-Atlantic cooperation, and called for a "United States of Europe."

During his long public career, Churchill served six monarchs,

Contents

Introduction

Sir Winston Churchill's words defined the political landscape of an era—and forever changed the course of human history. The eloquence and passion of his wartime speeches galvanised the British nation in its heroic stand against the Nazi aggression that had brought the Continent to its knees, and rallied people from all corners of

fought in battles on four continents, and served 62 years in Parliament, holding Cabinet offices such as Undersecretary of State for the Colonies, Home Secretary, and First Lord of the Admiralty, in addition to his two terms as Prime Minister. Further, Churchill wrote 42 volumes of history, memoir, essays, and collected works, a myriad of journalistic articles, and countless speeches, for which he never employed a speechwriter. For his service to the crown and to the world, he was named a Knight of the Garter; for his service to the world of letters, he was awarded the Nobel Prize for Literature.

To merely list Churchill's tremendous achievements, however, would not fully illuminate the breadth of his experiences and interests. As well as soldier, statesman, and orator, he was a talented painter, a successful sportsman, and a unionised stonemason. He was not only a great writer, but moreover a great wit: "In my behalf," he once said, "you cannot deal with the most serious things in the world unless you can understand the most amusing."

For this reason, the editors have included an ample array of Sir Winston's wisdom, ridiculous and sublime, in the pages that follow, so that all may enjoy the heart, humour, and humanity of the man who changed the world.

Biography

In 2002 the BBC conducted a poll among the people of the United Kingdom, asking them to name the greatest individuals in British history for the series *100 Greatest Britons*. Winston Churchill ranked first. In roles as a soldier, statesman, Nobel Prize-winning author, artist, and political leader during the darkest days of the twentieth century, Churchill's words and actions shaped the course of history and inspired not only British subjects but people all over the world.

He made his greatest mark on the world as Britain's prime minister, but Churchill's ancestors were from both sides of the Atlantic. His father, Lord Randolph Churchill, married American socialite Jennie Jerome and they had their first son, Winston Leonard Spencer Churchill, on November 30, 1874. For the rest of his life one of Winston's greatest inspirations to achieve and make a difference in the world was to honor the memory of his father, who died when Winston was only twenty-one.

Young Winston was educated at schools including St. George's and the Harrow. He had a rather restless spirit and did not complete his studies with the stellar academic record one might expect. Three attempts at the entrance exam gained Churchill entrance to Sandhurst, the prestigious Royal Military Academy, in 1893. After graduation Churchill became a Second Lieutenant in the Queen's Hussars. Early in his days as a soldier Churchill took up work as a war correspondent, reporting on battles for London newspapers, where the public first took notice of Churchill's writing.

As a soldier Churchill saw active service in lands as far-flung as India, Cuba, Cairo, and South Africa. He distinguished himself among officers and earned numerous honors and medals.

Churchill gained a seat in Parliament as a member of the Conservative Party in 1900. He held a multitude of positions and titles over the years and switched from conservative to "radical" liberal and back again, all the while earning the respect and admiration of fellow politicians and British subjects for his crusades to better his nation. As

Home Secretary Churchill supported liberal reforms and was instrumental in establishing the British welfare state. After becoming First Lord of the Admiralty in 1911 he concentrated his efforts on improving Royal Navy combat operations. In the midst of this activity, Churchill continued service in the military and managed a home life including marriage to Clementine Hozier, whom he had met at a dinner party in 1904. Their marriage in 1908 was followed by the birth of their five children, spread throughout the next fourteen years.

Early into the First World War, Churchill's reputation took a hit after a failed campaign in the Dardenelles. He resigned from his post and again joined the British forces in battle as a commander in the Grenadier Guards and later the Royal Scots Fusiliers. Churchill returned to politics in 1917 as Minister of Munitions and later Secretary of State for War, for Air, and for the Colonies. His notable actions during this time include creating the Anglo-Irish Treaty giving Ireland independence, establishing the boundaries of the modern Middle East, intervention in the Bolshevik Revolution, and demobilizing British troops at the conclusion of World War I.

In 1924 Prime Minister Stanley Baldwin appointed Churchill Chancellor of the Exchequer. During his tenure in this position he oversaw a return to the pre-war exchange rate and the Gold Standard, which led to a severe economic crisis and rampant unemployment. Churchill lost his seat when the Conservatives fell out of power in the general election of 1929. He also clashed with Prime Minister Baldwin on the subject of independence for India and did not hold office under Baldwin.

These were Churchill's "wilderness years," the nadir of his political career. Though out of power, Churchill continued to spread his world views, thoughts, and ideas through speeches, articles, and books.

During Churchill's period in the wilderness, Fascist leadership spread across Europe led by German Chancellor Adolf Hitler.

Churchill spoke out against policies of appeasement toward dictatorships. As Britain declared war on Germany on September 3, 1939, Churchill became First Lord of the Admiralty under Prime Minister Neville Chamberlain. After Chamberlain resigned, King George VI asked Churchill to become the Empire's Prime Minister.

The World War II years were Churchill's "finest hour" and forever cemented his position as a purveyor of strength and will against the forces of tyranny. Churchill led the charge against Hitler and the Axis forces at the height of their power. His rousing speeches became legendary for electrifying the Allied nations and inspiring them to continue the fight, even as nation after nation fell to the Axis forces and Britain endured nightly bombings. In 1941, the United States entered the war, strengthening the Allied arms. Churchill's strong alliance with national leaders, including United States President Franklin D. Roosevelt and France's Charles de Gaulle, united the nations when they needed support the most.

Though in his late sixties and suffering at times from poor health, Churchill worked tirelessly in opposition to Hitler. He traveled at risk of his life over 100,000 miles for negotiations with the leaders of other nations and worked to establish plans that would continue the war until the "unconditional surrender" of Germany. War raged on into

1944 and 1945, but by then the Allied forces were dominant. The Battle of Normandy marked a turning point by sending the Axis soldiers out of France and back into Germany. Germany surrendered on May 7, 1945, followed by Japan on August 15.

Though Churchill was immensely popular, the public thirsted for a clean slate—a

change of government to lead
them out of wartime. The Labour
Party came to power and
Churchill became leader of the
opposition, a role in which he
continued to have enormous
influence through to 1951, when
the Conservative Party was
restored to power. This period
was marked by Cold War tensions
with Russia, a problem which

Churchill famously named the "Iron Curtain." Churchill had suffered numerous heart attacks and strokes during the 1940s and '50s. Then entering his eighties, he resigned as prime minister in April 1955 and was succeeded by Anthony Eden.

In "retirement" Churchill continued to be active and was revered as a world leader who had seen his nation through its darkest times. Churchill passed away following a stroke in January 1965, at the age of ninety. Britain's most honored prime minister was given a state funeral attended by Queen Elizabeth herself as a sign of his standing in the annals of British history. Half a century after his death, Winston Churchill remains a symbol of leadership and courage. His words live on to inspire generation after generation to maintain "a lion's heart" in the face of adversity.

Churchill on Life

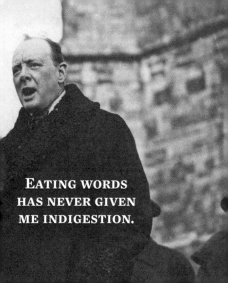

EATING WORDS
HAS NEVER GIVEN
ME INDIGESTION.

By being so long in the lowest form [at Harrow School] I gained an immense advantage over the cleverer boys. They all went on to learn Latin and Greek and splendid things like that. But I was taught English. . . . Thus I got into my bones the essential structure of the British sentence—which is a noble thing.

Headmasters have powers at their disposal with which Prime Ministers have never yet been invested.

Personally
I am always
willing to learn,
although I do
not always like
being taught.

A fanatic is
one who can't
change his
mind and
won't change
the subject.

It is a fine thing to be honest, but it is also very important to be right.

It is better to be making the news
than taking it, to be an actor
rather than a critic.

An appeaser is one who feeds a crocodile—hoping it will eat him last.

Don't argue
about the
difficulties.
The difficulties
will argue
for themselves.

NOTE TO AN EDITOR SCOLDING HIM
NOT TO END A SENTENCE WITH
A PREPOSITION:

This is the sort of impertinence up
with which I will not put.

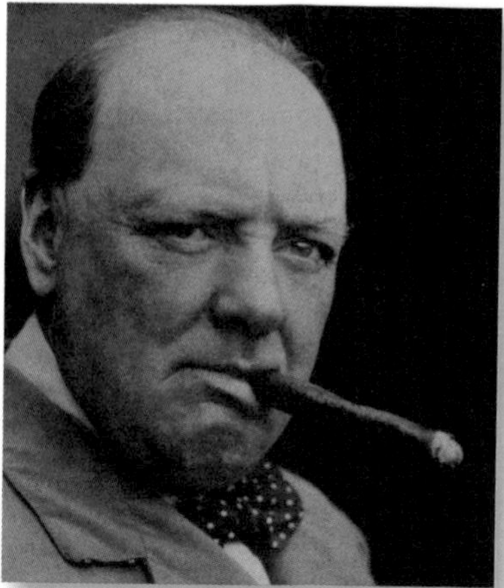

I must point out that my rule of life prescribes as an absolutely sacred rite smoking cigars and also the drinking of alcohol before, after, and if need be during all meals and in the intervals between them.

When I was younger I made it a rule never to take strong drink before lunch. It is now my rule never to do so before breakfast.

All I can say
is that I have
taken more out
of alcohol than
alcohol has taken
out of me.

LADY NANCY ASTOR:

Winston, if you were my husband, I'd put arsenic in your morning coffee.

CHURCHILL:

Madam, if you were my wife, I'd drink it.

BESSIE BRADDOCK:

Winston, you are drunk!

CHURCHILL:

And Madam, you are ugly.
And tomorrow, I'll be sober,
and you will still be ugly.

I t is hard, if not impossible, to snub
   a beautiful woman—they remain
beautiful and the rebuke recoils.

The price
of greatness
is responsibility.

Courage is rightly esteemed
the first of human qualities . . .
because it is the quality that
guarantees all others.

Churchill
at War

I have nothing to offer but blood, toil, tears, and sweat.

To Prime Minister Neville
Chamberlain, following the
Munich agreement:

You were given a choice between
war and dishonor. You have chosen
dishonor and you will have war.

Y ou ask, what is our policy? I will say: it is to wage war, by sea, land, and air, with all our might. . . . You ask, what is our aim? I can answer in one word: victory . . . . Victory at all costs, victory in spite of all terror, victory however long and hard the road may be; for without victory there is no survival!

—*First statement as Prime Minister*

We shall not flag or fail. We shall go on to the end, we shall fight in France, we shall fight on the seas and oceans, we shall fight with growing confidence and growing strength in the air, we shall defend our Island whatever the cost, we shall fight on the landing grounds, we shall fight in the fields and in the streets, we shall fight in the hills; we shall never surrender.

—*Speech following the Dunkirk evacuation*

Let us therefore brace
ourselves to our duties, and
so bear ourselves that if the
British Empire and its
Commonwealth last for a
thousand years, men will still say:
'This was their finest hour'.

—*Speech before the Battle of Britain*

Never in the field of human conflict was so much owed by so many to so few.

*—Tribute to the Royal Air Force
following the Battle of Britain*

Death and sorrow will be the companions of our journey; hardship our garment; constancy and valor our only shield. We must be united, we must be undaunted, we must be inflexible.

[In war] the
latest refinements
of science are linked
with the cruelties
of the Stone Age.

ON THE PARACHUTE LANDING
OF RUDOLF HESS IN SCOTLAND:

This is one of those cases in which the imagination is baffled by the facts.

ON THE NAZI INVASION OF THE
SOVIET UNION:

If Hitler invaded Hell I would make at least a favourable reference to the Devil in the House of Commons.

To Adolf Hitler:

We will have no
truce or parley with
you, or the grisly gang
who do your wicked will.
You do your worst—and
we will do our best.

The V sign is the symbol of the unconquerable will of the occupied territories, and a portent of the fate awaiting the Nazi tyranny.

Do not let us speak of darker days; let us speak rather of sterner days. These are not dark days: these are great days—the greatest days our country has ever lived; and we must thank God that we have been allowed, each of us according to our stations, to play a part in making these days memorable in the history of our race.

When I was called
upon to be Prime Minister,
now nearly two years ago,
there were not many
applicants for the job.
Since then perhaps the
market has improved.

ON THE VICTORY AT EL ALAMEIN:

This is not the end.
It is not even the beginning
of the end. But it is,
perhaps, the end
of the beginning.

In wartime, truth is so precious
that she should always be
attended by a bodyguard of lies.

'Not in vain' may be the pride of those who survived and the epitaph of those who fell.

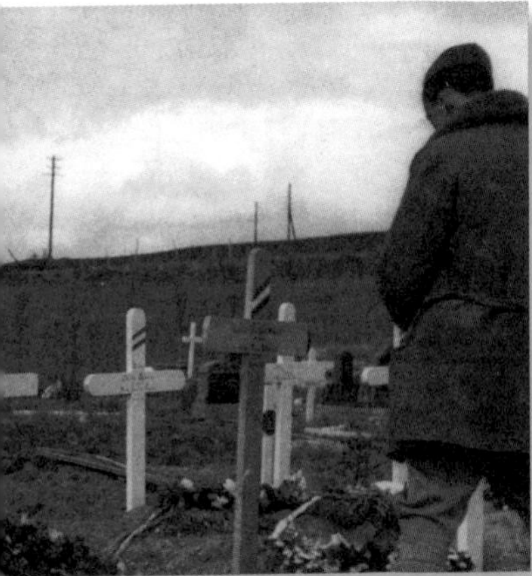

The nation had the lion's heart. I had the luck to give the roar.

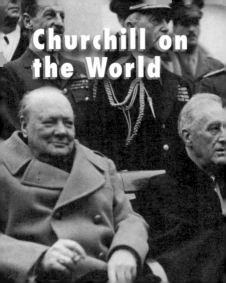

Churchill on
the World

The reason for having diplomatic relations is not to confer a compliment, but to secure a convenience.

On the office of Prime Minister:

If he trips he must be sustained; if he makes mistakes they must be covered; if he sleeps he must not be wantonly disturbed; if he is no good he must be poleaxed.

I do not resent
criticism, even when,
for the sake of
emphasis, it parts for
the time with reality.

ON DECLINING KNIGHTHOOD
FOLLOWING THE TORY DEFEAT
AT THE POLLS:

I could not receive the Order of the Garter from my sovereign when I received the order of the boot from his people.

Political ability: It is the ability to foretell what is going to happen tomorrow, next week, next month and next year. And to have the ability afterward to explain why it didn't happen.

ON THE SOVIET UNION:

I cannot forecast to
you the action of
Russia. It is a riddle
wrapped in a mystery
inside an enigma.

I always avoid prophesying
beforehand, because it is much
better policy to prophesy after the
event has already taken place.

The English
never draw a
line without
blurring it.

The Almighty in His infinite wisdom did not see fit to create Frenchmen in the image of Englishmen.

GAS MASK FITTING HERE

NOW IN

The maxim of the British people is 'Business as usual'.

The practice of Parliament must be judged by quality, not quantity. You cannot judge the passing of laws by Parliament as you would judge the output of an efficient Chicago bacon factory.

Democracy is
the worst system
devised by wit
of man, except
for all the others.

Dictators ride to and fro upon tigers which they dare not dismount. And the tigers are getting hungry.

Some Socialists see private enterprise as a tiger—a predatory target to be shot. Others see it as an old cow to be milked. But we Conservatives see it as the sturdy horse that pulls along our economy.

The inherent vice
of capitalism is
the unequal sharing
of blessings; the
inherent virtue of
socialism is the equal
sharing of miseries.

It is the socialist
idea that making
profits is a vice;
I consider the real
vice is making losses.

ON SOCIALISM:

Government of the duds, by the duds and for the duds.

Churchill and His Contemporaries

On Elizabeth II: Lovely, inspiring. All the film people in the world if they

had scoured the globe
could not have found any-
one so suited to the part.

ON PRIME MINISTER
JAMES RAMSEY MACDONALD:

We know that he has,
more than any other man,
the gift of compressing
the largest number of
words into the smallest
amount of thought.

106

ON THE ADMINISTRATION OF
PRIME MINISTER STANLEY BALDWIN:

Decided only to be undecided, resolved to be irresolute, adamant for drift, solid for fluidity, all-powerful to be impotent.

ON VLADIMIR LENIN:

His sympathies cold and wide as the Arctic Ocean; his hatreds tight as the hangman's noose. His purpose to save the world: his method to blow it up.

ON PRIME MINISTER
NEVILLE CHAMBERLAIN:

He looked at foreign affairs through the wrong end of a municipal drainpipe.

On Sir Richard Stafford Cripps:

There, but for the grace of God, goes God.

ON SIR RICHARD
STAFFORD CRIPPS:

He has all of
the virtues I dislike
and none of the
vices I admire.

None of his colleagues can compare with him in that acuteness of energy of mind with which he devotes himself to so many topics injurious to the strength and welfare of the State.

On Edward F. Wood,
Earl of Halifax:

Halifax's virtues have done more
harm in the world than the
vices of hundreds of other people.

ON MINISTER OF HEALTH
ANEURIN BEVAN:

I can think of no better step to
signalise the inauguration of the
National Health Service than that a
person who so obviously needs
psychiatric attention should be
among the first of its patients.

ON FIELD MARSHAL BERNARD 'MONTY' MONTGOMERY, ALLIED COMMANDER:

ndomitable in retreat; invincible in advance; insufferable in victory.

ON CHARLES DE GAULLE:

Of all the crosses
I have to bear, the
heaviest is the
Cross of Lorraine.

ON CHARLES DE GAULLE:

England's grievous offence in de Gaulle's eyes is that she has helped France. He cannot bear to think that she needed help. He will not relax his vigilance in guarding her honour for a single instant.

ON JOHN FOSTER DULLES,
U.S. SECRETARY OF STATE:

He is the only case
I know of a bull who
carries around his own
china shop with him.

ON PRIME MINISTER CLEMENT ATTLEE:

He is a sheep in sheep's clothing.

Mr. Attlee is a very modest man.
But then he has much to be
modest about.

EULOGY FOR
FRANKLIN D. ROOSEVELT:

He died in harness, and we may well say in battle harness, like his soldiers, sailors, and airmen who died side by side with ours in carrying out their tasks to the end all over the world. What an enviable death was his.

Churchill at Last

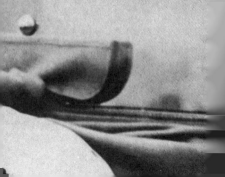

The greatest lesson in
life is to know that even
fools are right
sometimes.

Politics are almost as exciting as war, and quite as dangerous. In war you can only be killed once, but in politics many times.

DEFINITION OF A POLITICIAN:

He is asked to
stand, he wants
to sit, he is
expected to lie.

An optimist
sees an opportunity
in every calamity;
a pessimist sees
a calamity in
every opportunity.

am an optimist. It does not seem
too much use being anything else.

True genius resides in the capacity for the evaluation of uncertain, hazardous, and conflicting information.

S hort words are best and the old words when short are best of all.

Personally, I like
short words and
vulgar fractions.

No one can
guarantee success
in war, but only
deserve it.

Never give in, never give in, never, never, never, never—in nothing, great or small, large or petty—never give in except to convictions of honour and good sense.

ON THE REBUILDING OF THE
HOUSE OF COMMONS:

We shape our buildings;
thereafter they shape us.

One ought to be just
before one is generous.

Men occasionally stumble over the truth, but most of them pick themselves up and hurry off as if nothing had happened.

Writing a book is an adventure. To begin with, it is a toy and an amusement. Then it becomes a mistress, then it becomes a master, then it becomes a tyrant. The last phase is that just as you are about to be reconciled to your servitude, you kill the monster, and fling him to the public.

Out of intense complexities
intense simplicities emerge.

For my part, I consider that it will be found much better by all parties to leave the past to history, especially as I propose to write that history myself.

If the human race wishes to have a prolonged and indefinite period of material prosperity, they have only got to behave in a peaceful and helpful way toward one another, and science will do for them all they wish and more than they can dream.

We are happier in
many ways when we
are old than when we
were young. The young
sow wild oats, the
old grow sage.

When I look back on all these worries I remember the story of the old man who said on his deathbed that he had had a lot of trouble in his life, most of which never happened.

The farther
backward you can
look, the farther
forward you are
likely to see.

In War: Resolution.
In Defeat: Defiance.
In Victory: Magnanimity.
In Peace: Good Will.

MAY 13, 1940:
CHURCHILL'S FIRST SPEECH
TO THE HOUSE OF COMMONS
AS PRIME MINISTER OF THE
BRITISH EMPIRE

I beg to move, that this House welcomes the formation of a Government representing the united and inflexible resolve of the nation to prosecute the war with Germany to a victorious conclusion.

On Friday evening last I received His Majesty's commission to form a new Administration. It is the evident wish and will of Parliament and the nation that this should be conceived on the broadest possible basis and that it should include all parties, both those who supported the late Government and also the parties of the Opposition. I have com-

pleted the most important part of
this task. A War Cabinet has been
formed of five Members, representing, with the Opposition Liberals,
the unity of the nation. The three
party Leaders have agreed to
serve, either in the War Cabinet
or in high executive office. The
three Fighting Services have been
filled. It was necessary that this
should be done in one single day,

on account of the extreme urgency and rigor of events. A number of other positions, key positions, were filled yesterday, and I am submitting a further list to His Majesty tonight. I hope to complete the appointment of the principal Ministers during tomorrow. The appointment of the other Ministers usually takes a little longer, but I trust that, when

Parliament meets again, this part of my task will be completed, and that the administration will be complete in all respects.

I considered it in the public interest to suggest that the House should be summoned to meet today. Mr. Speaker agreed, and took the necessary steps, in accordance with the powers conferred upon him by the Resolution of the

House. At the end of the pro-
ceedings today, the Adjournment of
the House will be proposed until
Tuesday, 21st May, with, of course,
provision for earlier meeting, if
need be. The business to be
considered during that week will be
notified to Members at the earliest
opportunity. I now invite the
House, by the Motion which stands
in my name, to record its approval

of the steps taken and to declare its confidence in the new Government.

To form an Administration of this scale and complexity is a serious undertaking in itself, but it must be remembered that we are in the preliminary stage of one of the greatest battles in history, that we are in action at many other points in Norway and in

Holland, that we have to be prepared in the Mediterranean, that the air battle is continuous, and that many preparations, such as have been indicated by my honorable friend below the Gangway, have to be made here at home. In this crisis I hope I may be pardoned if I do not address the House at any length today. I hope that any of my friends and colleagues, or former colleagues, who are affected by the political reconstruction, will make allowance, all allowance, for any lack of ceremony with which it has been necessary to act. I would say to the House, as I said to those who have joined this government: I have nothing to offer but blood, toil, tears, and sweat.

We have before us an ordeal

of the most grievous kind. We
have before us many, many long
months of struggle and of suffering. You ask, what is our
policy? I can say: It is to wage war,
by sea, land, and air, with all our
might and with all the strength
that God can give us; to wage war
against a monstrous tyranny,
never surpassed in the dark,
lamentable catalog of human

crime. That is our policy. You ask, what is our aim? I can answer in one word. It is: Victory. Victory at all costs. Victory in spite of all terror. Victory, however long and hard the road may be; for without victory, there is no survival. Let that be realised; no survival for the British Empire, no survival for all that the British Empire has stood for, no survival for the urge and impulse of the ages, that mankind will move forward towards its goal. But I take up my task with buoyancy and hope. I feel sure that our cause will not be suffered to fail among men. At this time I feel entitled to claim the aid of all, and I say: Come then, let us go forward together with our united strength.

JUNE 4, 1940: EXCERPT FROM
CHURCHILL'S SPEECH TO THE
HOUSE OF COMMONS

Turning once again, and this time more generally, to the question of invasion, I would observe that there has never been a period in all these long centuries of which we boast when an absolute guarantee against invasion, still less against serious raids, could have been given to our people. In the days of Napoleon the same wind which would have carried his transports across the Channel might have driven away the blockading fleet. There was always the chance, and it is that chance which has excited and befooled the imaginations of many Continental tyrants. Many are the tales that are told. We are assured that novel methods will be adopted, and when we see the originality of malice, the ingenuity of aggression, which our enemy displays, we may certainly prepare ourselves for every kind of novel stratagem and every kind of brutal and treacherous maneuver. I think that no idea is so outlandish that it should not be considered and viewed with a searching, but at the same time, I hope, with a steady eye. We must never forget the solid assurances of sea power and those which belong to air power if it can be locally exercised.

I have, myself, full confidence that if all do their duty, if nothing is neglected, and if the best arrangements are made, as they are being made, we shall prove ourselves once again able to defend our Island home, to ride out the storm of war, and to outlive the menace of tyranny, if necessary for years, if necessary alone. At any rate, that is what we are going to try to do. That is the resolve of His Majesty's Government—every man of them. That is the will of Parliament and the nation. The British Empire and the French Republic, linked together in their cause and in their need, will defend to the death their native soil, aiding each other like good comrades to the utmost of their strength. Even though large tracts of Europe and many old and famous States have fallen or may fall into the grip of the Gestapo and all the odious apparatus of Nazi rule, we shall not flag or fail. We shall go on to the end. We shall fight in France, we shall fight on the seas and oceans, we shall fight with growing confidence and growing strength in the air, we shall defend our Island, whatever the cost may be. We shall fight on the beaches, we shall fight on the landing grounds, we shall fight in the fields and in the streets, we shall fight in the hills. We shall never surrender, and even if, which I do not for a moment believe, this Island or a large part of it were subjugated and starving, then our Empire beyond the seas, armed and guarded by the British Fleet, would carry on the struggle, until, in God's good time, the New World, with all its power and might, steps forth to the rescue and the liberation of the old.

During the first four years of the last war the Allies experienced nothing but disaster and disappointment. That was our constant fear: one blow after another, terrible losses, frightful dangers. Everything miscarried. And yet at the end of those four years the morale of the Allies was higher than that of the Germans, who had moved from one aggressive triumph to another, and who stood everywhere triumphant invaders of the lands into which they had broken. During that war we repeatedly asked ourselves the question: How are we going to win? And no one was able ever to answer it with much precision, until at the end, quite suddenly, quite unexpectedly, our terrible foe collapsed before us, and we were so glutted with victory that in our folly we threw it away.

We do not yet know what will happen in France or whether the French resistance will be prolonged, both in France and in the French Empire overseas. The

French Government will be throwing away great opportunities and casting adrift their future if they do not continue the war in accordance with their Treaty obligations, from which we have not felt able to release them. The House will have read the historic declaration in which, at the desire of many Frenchmen— and of our own hearts—we have proclaimed our willingness at the darkest hour in French history to conclude a union of common citizenship in this struggle. However matters may go in France or with the French Government, or other French Governments, we in this Island and in the British Empire will never lose our sense of comradeship with the French people.

If we are now called upon to endure what they have been suffering, we shall emulate their courage, and if final victory rewards our toils they shall share the gains and freedom shall be restored to all. We abate nothing of our just demands; not one jot or tittle do we recede. Czechs, Poles, Norwegians, Dutch, Belgians have joined their causes to our own. All these shall be restored.

What General Weygand called the Battle of France is over. I expect that the Battle of Britain is about to begin. Upon this battle depends the survival of Christian civilization. Upon it depends our own British life, and the long continuity of our institutions and our Empire. The whole fury and might of the enemy must very soon be turned on us. Hitler knows that he will have to break us in this Island or lose the war. If we can stand up to him, all Europe may be free and the life of the world may move forward into broad, sunlit uplands. But if we fail, then the whole world, including the United States, including all that we have known and cared for, will sink into the abyss of a new Dark Age made more sinister, and perhaps more protracted, by the lights of perverted science. Let us therefore brace ourselves to our duties, and so bear ourselves that, if the British Empire and its Commonwealth last for a thousand years, men will still say: "This was their finest hour."

MARCH 5, 1946:
EXCERPTS FROM CHURCHILL'S ADDRESS
AT WESTMINSTER COLLEGE
IN FULTON, MISSOURI

From Stettin in the Baltic to Trieste in the Adriatic, an iron curtain has descended across the Continent. Behind that line lie all the capitals of the ancient states of Central and Eastern Europe. Warsaw, Berlin, Prague, Vienna,

Budapest, Belgrade, Bucharest and Sofia, all these famous cities and the populations around them lie in what I must call the Soviet sphere, and all are subject in one form or another, not only to Soviet influence but to a very high and, in many cases, increasing measure of control from Moscow.

. . .The safety of the world requires a new unity in Europe,

from which no nation should be
permanently outcast. It is from
the quarrels of the strong parent
races in Europe that the world
wars we have witnessed, or which
occurred in former times, have
sprung. Twice in our own lifetime
we have seen the United States,
against their wishes and their
traditions, against arguments, the
force of which it is impossible not

to comprehend, drawn by irresistible forces, into these wars in time to secure the victory of the good cause, but only after frightful slaughter and devastation had occurred. Twice the United States has had to send several millions of its young men across the Atlantic to find the war; but now war can find any nation, wherever it may dwell between dusk and dawn. Surely we should work with conscious purpose for a grand pacification of Europe, within the structure of the United Nations and in accordance with its Charter. That I feel is an open cause of policy of very great importance.

In front of the iron curtain which lies across Europe are other causes for anxiety. In Italy the

Communist Party is seriously hampered by having to support the Communist-trained Marshal Tito's claims to former Italian territory at the head of the Adriatic. Nevertheless the future of Italy hangs in the balance. Again one cannot imagine a regenerated Europe without a strong France. All my public life I have worked for a Strong France and I never lost faith in her destiny, even in the darkest hours. I will not lose faith now. However, in a great number of countries, far from the Russian frontiers and throughout the world, Communist fifth columns are established and work in complete unity and absolute obedience to the directions they receive from the Communist center. Except in the British Commonwealth and in the United States, where Communism is in its infancy, the Communist parties or fifth columns constitute a growing challenge and peril to Christian civilization. These are somber facts for anyone to have to recite on the morrow of a victory gained by so much splendid comradeship in arms and in the cause of freedom and democracy; but we should be most unwise not to face them squarely while time remains.

The outlook is also anxious in the Far East and especially in Manchuria. The Agreement which was made at Yalta, to which I was a party, was extremely favorable to Soviet Russia, but it was made at a time when no one could say that the German war might not extend all through the summer and autumn of 1945 and when the Japanese war was expected to last for a further eighteen months from the end of the German war. In this country you are all so well-informed about the Far East, and such devoted friends of China, that I do not need to expatiate on the situation there.

I have felt bound to portray
the shadow which, alike in the
west and in the east, falls upon
the world. I was a high minister at
the time of the Versailles Treaty
and a close friend of Mr. Lloyd-
George, who was the head of the
British delegation at Versailles. I
did not myself agree with many
things that were done, but I have
a very strong impression in my

mind of that situation, and I find it painful to contrast it with that which prevails now. In those days there were high hopes and unbounded confidence that the wars were over, and that the League of Nations would become all-powerful. I do not see or feel that same confidence or even the same hopes in the haggard world at the present time.

On the other hand I repulse the idea that a new war is inevitable; still more that it is imminent. It is because I am sure that our fortunes are still in our own hands and that we hold the power to save the future, that I feel the duty to speak out now that I have the occasion and the opportunity to do so. I do not believe that Soviet Russia desires war. What they desire is the fruits of war and the indefinite expansion of their power and doctrines. But what we have to consider here today while time remains, is the permanent prevention of war and the establishment of conditions of freedom and democracy as rapidly as possible in all countries. Our difficulties and dangers will not be removed by closing our eyes to them. They will not be removed by mere waiting to see what happens; nor will they be removed by a policy of appeasement. What is needed is a settlement, and the longer this is delayed, the more difficult it will be and the greater our dangers will become.

. . .Last time I saw it all

coming and cried aloud to my own fellow-countrymen and to the world, but no one paid any attention. Up till the year 1933 or even 1935, Germany might have been saved from the awful fate which has overtaken her and we might all have been spared the miseries Hitler let loose upon mankind. There never was a war in all history easier to prevent by timely action than the one which has just desolated such great areas of the globe. It could have been prevented in my belief without the firing of a single shot, and Germany might be powerful, prosperous, and honored today; but no one would listen and one by one we were all sucked into the awful whirlpool. We surely must not let that happen again. This can only be achieved by reaching now, in 1946, a good understanding on all points with Russia under the general authority of the United Nations Organization and by the maintenance of that good understanding through many peaceful years, by the world instrument, supported by the whole strength of the English-speaking world and all its connections.

There is the solution which I respectfully offer to you in this Address to which I have given the title "The Sinews of Peace."

Let no man underrate the abiding power of the British Empire and Commonwealth. Because you see the 46 millions in our Island harassed about their food supply, of which they only grow one half, even in war-time, or because we have difficulty in restarting our industries and export trade after six years of passionate war effort. Do not suppose that we shall not come through these dark years of privation as we have come through the glorious years of agony, or that half a century from now, you will not see seventy or eighty millions of Britons spread about the world and united in defense of our traditions, our way of life, and of the world causes which you and we espouse. If the population of the English-speaking Commonwealths be added to that of the United States with all that such cooperation implies in the air, on the sea, all over the globe, and in science and in industry, and in moral force, there will be no quivering, precarious balance of power to offer its temptation to ambition or adventure. On the contrary, there will be an overwhelming assurance of security. If we adhere faithfully to the Charter of the United Nations and walk forward in sedate and sober strength seeking no one's land or treasure, seeking to lay no arbitrary control upon the thoughts of men; if all British moral and material forces and convictions are joined with your own in fraternal association, the high-roads of the future will be clear, not only for us but for all, not only for our time, but for a century to come. ■

PHOTOGRAPHY CREDITS

This book has been bound using handcraft methods, and is
Smyth-sewn to ensure durability.

The cover was designed by Bill Jones.

The interior was
designed by Toni Renée Leslie
and Bill Jones.

The text was edited
by Brendan J. Cahill and Jennifer
Leczkowski.

Photo research was executed
by Susan Oyama.

The text was set in
Mercury and Futura.